The Little Book of Kombucha

Best Delicious Kombucha Recipes, Useful Tips & Tricks, Most Common Mistakes

By: Kevin Curt

© Copyright 2017 by Kevin Curt - All rights reserved.

This document is geared towards providing exact and reliable information in regards to the topic and issue covered. The publication is sold with the idea that the publisher is not required to render accounting, officially permitted, or otherwise, qualified services. If advice is necessary, legal or professional, a practiced individual in the profession should be ordered.

From a Declaration of Principles which was accepted and approved equally by a Committee of the American Bar Association and a Committee of Publishers and Associations.

In no way is it legal to reproduce, duplicate, or transmit any part of this document in either electronic means or in printed format. Recording of this publication is strictly prohibited and any storage of this document is not allowed unless with written permission from the publisher. All rights reserved.

The information provided herein is stated to be truthful and consistent, in that any liability, in terms of inattention or otherwise, by any usage or abuse of any policies, processes, or directions contained within is the solitary and utter responsibility of the recipient reader. Under no circumstances will any legal responsibility or blame be held against the publisher for any reparation, damages, or monetary loss due to the information herein, either directly or indirectly. Respective authors own all copyrights not held by the publisher. The information herein is offered for informational purposes solely, and is universal as so. The presentation of the information is without contract or any type of guarantee assurance.

The trademarks that are used are without any consent, and the publication of the trademark is without permission or backing by the trademark owner. All trademarks and brands within this book are for clarifying purposes only and are the owned by the owners themselves, not affiliated with this document.

Table of Contents

Introduction 1

Chapter One: Kombucha 101 2

What is the deal with Kombucha? 3

Why do people care? 4

History 7
- Is Kombucha an ancient Chinese secret? 7

Chapter Two: Benefits of Kombucha 11

Kombucha contains probiotics 11

Contains the benefits of green tea 12

Kombucha contains antioxidants 12

Kombucha can kill bacteria 13

Reduce Risk of Heart Diseases 13

Prevent Type II Diabetes 13

Kombucha can help to prevent cancer 14

Chapter Three: Debunking the myths 15

Kombucha is a mushroom 15

Metal affects the brewing process 15

Kombucha creates acidity 16

Home Brewing is unsafe 17

Kombucha cures all 17

Chapter Four: How to Brew Kombucha......18

Brewing Kombucha 18

Kombucha Ratios 19

Common Mistakes made...22
    Storing Kombucha in direct sunlight..................................22
    Rinsing SCOBY...22
    Refrigerating SCOBY..22
    Using Weak Starter Tea..23
    Oversteeping Tea..23

Tips to Making Good Kombucha 24

Chapter Three: Kombucha Recipes............25

Ginger and Blueberry Kombucha 26

Ginger and Lemon Kombucha 29

Chocolate and Strawberry Kombucha 32

Virgin Mojito Kombucha...35

Pumpkin Kombucha..38

Cinnamon and Apple Kombucha 41

Chia Seed Kombucha..43

Cayenne and Pineapple Kombucha 45

Basil with a Twist 48

Raspberry and Lemon Kombucha..........................51

Orange Kombucha...54

Conclusion 57

Introduction

I want to thank you for choosing this book, *'The Little book of Kombucha'*

Kombucha is a type of fermented tea that is made from either green or black tea, sugar, bacteria and yeast culture. This drink has taken the world by storm because of the multiple benefits it provides. People who are looking for a different way to lose weight can try drinking this tea instead of green tea or black tea. The book details the multiple benefits provided by the brew.

Kombucha may seem difficult to brew yourself, especially when you are starting out. Particular ingredients, quantities, storage conditions and brewing conditions are information that will overwhelm you and may discourage you if you are a newbie. This book covers some basic steps that will make it easy for you to get your first cup of kombucha right. It also focuses on some aspects of brewing kombucha that every beginner must know. You will find that the steps mentioned in the book are easy to follow.

Thank you for purchasing the book. I hope you gather all the information you are looking for about kombucha.

Chapter One: Kombucha 101

What do you mix with tea – sugar or tea? Why not try some bacteria? Kombucha is a concoction of tea, sugar and bacteria that is having its time to shine. People who drink this tea have been talking about how their health has improved over time. This drink is said to have the taste and smell of vinegar and has been described as being everything - right from fizzy apples to rotten apples. Do you believe this drink can solve all your ailments? Let us take a look at the different aspects of kombucha before you take your first sip.

What is the deal with Kombucha?

Kombucha is not a new drink on the market, although it has only gained popularity now. This tea was first consumed by the Chinese, close to 2000 years ago, to treat inflammatory ailments like arthritis and to even ward off diseases like cancer. Recently, kombucha has been used as a remedy that can be used to treat hypertension, constipation, fatigue, headaches and acne.

This drink is easy to make at home – all you need is sugar, tea, and some bacteria and yeast. The bacteria and yeast are active starter cultures that are alternatively known as "mother culture" which are combined with either green or black tea. This mixture is left to sit for ten days. A thin colony of bacteria is formed at the top of the mixture. Once the process of fermentation is complete, the culture formed on top can be scooped out while the drink below is ready to use. The scooped-out culture can be used to make other brews.

Why do people care?

Trendy restaurants and grocery stores have begun to feature fermented foods like kimchi, kefir, sauerkraut and kombucha. People from different spectrums of life, right from health nuts to chefs, are becoming aware of the benefits of eating foods that are rich in probiotics. Probiotics are similar to the bacteria that are present in the intestines. Research has concluded that probiotics help with fighting colds, reduce cholesterol in the blood, and promoting a healthy digestive system, thus alleviating issues like diarrhea, food allergies and irritable bowel syndrome.

The benefits of kombucha are impressive, but studies on the effects of the tea have been conducted only on rodents. However, the results prove that the tea does indeed provide all the benefits. One study concluded that rats that gulped this beverage down produced more antioxidants when put under extreme stress. They had less DNA damage when compared to the rats that did not consume the tea. It was observed that kombucha reversed the damaging effects of stress on the immune system. Similar research concluded that kombucha always maintained the level of antioxidants in rats that have been put under undue stress. Some experts have suggested that kombucha is rich in Vitamin B, which is known to maintain and regulate energy and stabilize metabolism thereby contributing to healthy skin and a healthy heart.

The benefits of the fermented tea are appealing, but those who make it at home tend to make a few mistakes that stir up concerns. Since there is a lot of bacteria floating around on the tea, if the fermented drink is left out in the open, it can get contaminated which can lead to an upset stomach or, in some instances, death. It is dangerous to make the tea in a ceramic container since the bacteria draw out the lead from that container, which contaminates the tea. Some tips and mistakes to avoid when making kombucha have been covered in detail in later chapters.

Some researchers are uncertain about the percentage of alcohol in the tea which is a by-product of fermentation, which is a process similar to the one used to make beer or wine. Whole Foods, in the year 2010, took some kombucha off the shelves since they were concerned that the kombucha continued to ferment even after it was packed. This increased the alcohol content in the kombucha. The labels and recipes were tweaked to reduce the alcohol content to 0.5 percent ABV (alcohol by volume). Some brews that contain more alcohol are sold to people over the age of 21. Since only four ounces of tea are recommended to be consumed regularly, the chances of feeling buzzed or getting drunk are slim. Most batches do start out with large cups of sugar; however, the sweet portion of the drink is fermented out thereby leaving only one or two grams of sugar per serving. It can be said that this brew has less sugar when compared to soda and other bottled or aerated drinks like lemonade, green tea, or other beverages.

History

Is Kombucha an ancient Chinese secret?

If you ask a hundred people what Kombucha is, 99 people may ask you what Kombucha is. But, if you were to ask one fan of kombucha what it is, you will definitely get a different answer. It is unfortunate that people are not aware of where the drink originated. However, it is known that kombucha has been around for years, maybe even centuries or millennia. There are a few stories of how kombucha came into existence.

One story is that the kombucha was invented for Emperor Qinshi Huangdi of the Qin Dynasty in 220BC. The Chinese are known to go on a quest to find an elixir that increases longevity. They have always looked towards nature to find ways to cure their ailments. This brew was called the tea of immortality in those times. However, it is now called stomach treasure, sea mushroom, or sea treasure. During the revolution, every house in China had a pot of Kombucha that was either brewing or ready to drink. But, it has fallen out of the routine in modern Chinese households.

Another story that has taken the rounds is that a Korean doctor, Dr. Kombu, brought the tea to a Japanese Emperor in 414AD. It was said that the warriors of ancient Japan, Samurais, used to carry this brew in their wine skins since it gave them immense amounts of energy. This is an explanation that may seem too easy, but Chinese and Japanese stories are the stuff of legends. The evidence to links of ancient China compels most people to believe this story.

There are some who believe that this vinegary, fermented beverage also filled the flasks of Genghis

Khan and his soldiers. These armies were also credited with inventing a form of cooking that is used across the world – barbecue and six people out of ten people likely to be direct descendants of Genghis Khan.

It traveled to Russia via the Silk Road and then to Europe from Asia. The first time the use of Kombucha was recorded in history was in the 19th century when it was used in Russia and Ukraine. This tea is called mushroom tea in Russia and was attributed to saving the life of Alexandre Solzhenitsyn's life when he was exiled in Siberia.

Kombucha was a popular drink until World War II in Europe and Russia, until tea and sugar were rationed. This made it hard for average families to purchase these ingredients. This makes it easy to understand why this practice was lost. Some people did preserve this tradition, and this drink was brewed in Italy for a few years before it began to be brewed in different households across Europe.

In the year 1960, the Swiss research team confirmed the benefits that one obtains on consuming kombucha. This gave rise to its popularity. Over the last few decades, the brew has become popular in the United States and Australia, especially since the early 2000s. There are health scares that occur occasionally, but there is no evidence that kombucha causes any illnesses. It is only the sloppy and improper brewing techniques that are to blame.

More research does need to be carried out on numerous topics that concern kombucha. Since this drink cannot be patented or controlled by any company, there is little money that is available to conduct clinical trials or wide-scale research. There is a research body that is being formed to understand the effects of kombucha better.

Chapter Two: Benefits of Kombucha

This section covers the benefits of kombucha that have been backed by scientific evidence.

Kombucha contains probiotics

As mentioned earlier, kombucha is a brew that is thought to have originated in Japan or China. This drink is made by adding some cultures of yeast, bacteria, and sugar to either green or black tea which is left to ferment for ten days. During the fermentation process, a mushroom-like blob is formed on the surface, which is used to ferment other kombucha brews. This blob is a SCOBY or a symbiotic colony of bacteria and yeast. During the process, vinegar, some acidic compounds, alcohol, and gases are produced that make the drink carbonated. The process also produced probiotics in large amounts. These bacteria are healthy and are similar to the bacteria found in the intestines. They improve our health by reducing inflammation, inducing weight loss, and by improving metabolism. If you consume kombucha regularly, you can improve your health.

Contains the benefits of green tea

Green tea is considered to be one of the healthiest drinks since it contains numerous bioactive compounds that work as antioxidants. Kombucha, when made from green tea, has similar chemical properties and therefore has some similar benefits. Research conducted on green tea has concluded that regular consumption increases the number of calories burnt, reduces belly fat, controls blood sugar levels and improves cholesterol levels. Some studies have concluded that green tea also helps to reduce the risk of prostate, colon, and breast cancers.

Kombucha contains antioxidants

Antioxidants are chemical compounds that fight reactive molecules and free radicals that cause cell damage. It is always better to supply antioxidants to your body through beverages and foods instead of antioxidant supplements. Kombucha, when made with green tea, has a powerful effect on the liver. Studies conducted on rats have concluded that drinking kombucha regularly helps with reducing liver damage by at least 70%. This cannot be said with certainty for human beings since it has not been tested on people with liver disease, but it is a promising area of research.

Kombucha can kill bacteria

A product that is produced during the process of fermentation is acetic acid, which is found in abundance in vinegar. This acid is known to kill harmful microorganisms. Kombucha, when made from either green or black tea, is known to have strong antibacterial properties that prevent the body from procuring any infections caused by bacteria or yeast. A study on chickens found that kombucha has similar effects as antibiotics – it had both growth-promoting and antimicrobial effects. Researchers also suggested that the tea could be consumed as an alternative to antibiotic growth-promoters that are fed to chickens.

Reduce Risk of Heart Diseases

One of the world's leading causes of death is heart disease. Research conducted on rats has concluded that kombucha can increases the levels of LDL and HDL cholesterol in the blood in less than 30 days. Green tea is known to prevent the oxidation of LDL cholesterol, which is a known contributor to heart disease. Drinking kombucha is said to decrease the risk of developing heart diseases by at least 31%.

Prevent Type II Diabetes

Type II diabetes is a disease that affects close to 300 million people across the globe. Insulin resistance and high blood sugar levels characterize this disease.

A study conducted on diabetic rats concluded that kombucha slowed the digestion of carbohydrates, thereby improving the functioning of the kidney and liver thereby reducing blood sugar levels. This brew, when made from green tea, is said to be more beneficial since green tea is known to reduce blood sugar levels. A study conducted on 300,000 subjects concluded that green tea helps with reducing the risk of procuring diabetes.

Kombucha can help to prevent cancer

One of the leading causes of death is cancer. This disease is characterized by the uncontrolled growth of mutated cells in the body. Kombucha helped prevent the growth of cancerous cells and also prevented them from spreading across the body if they were present in the body. This is because kombucha has a high concentration of antioxidants and polyphenols. How polyphenols work as anti-cancer agents is not a concept that is fully understood. It is thought that these compounds prevent the genes from mutating and block the formation of cancer cells, while also killing any cancer cells. Hence, it is not surprising that people who consume tea, especially green tea, are less likely to develop cancer.

Chapter Three: Debunking the myths

People have begun to gain interest in traditional methods of preparation and cultivation of food and also the fascination with making kombucha. However, when both excitement and ignorance are combined, facts are often jumbled leading to a number of myths making the rounds. Most information is harmless, but some myths confuse home brewers and lead to a disruption in proper brewing techniques. This chapter covers some myths that need to be debunked.

Kombucha is a mushroom

This belief is widely held since SCOBY resembles a mushroom. But, you will know by now that the culture used to brew kombucha is a symbiotic culture. It is true that mushroom and yeast are both fungi, and the cultures used to brew Kombucha is similar to the culture in mushrooms. This does not imply that the cultures are the same. To add to the confusion, some languages call kombucha mushroom tea.

Metal affects the brewing process

Since kombucha is known for its detoxifying properties, there are many people who mention that it is best to separate metal from kombucha. However, brief contact with a pair of scissors or a strainer will not make the kombucha toxic. The only metal that can be used to brew or store kombucha in is stainless steel grade 304 or higher. This is to prevent the leeching of certain toxic chemicals into the brew.

Kombucha creates acidity

The human body is a complex organism that maintains health through a process called homeostasis. Any shift in the internal pH indicates impending death or illness. To maintain a perfect pH, the body employs different buffering and detoxification systems that process the acids and reduce the residue that is generated due to the consumption of some food and also the by-products of some metabolic processes.

People are still debating over whether an acidic/alkaline diet is beneficial to health. It is known that food that is digested leaves residue in the body that is either alkaline or acidic in nature. It is because of this residue that the body is prone to producing disease-causing bacteria. It is important that you consume only one type of food over the other for every meal.

How does it work when it comes to kombucha? Will the reduction in pH values in the body create more acidity? Well, the answer is no. It is true that kombucha does have a low pH value, but the residue formed is alkaline rather than acidic and has an effect that is similar to apple cider vinegar or lemon juice.

Home Brewing is unsafe

When it comes to brewing kombucha at home, there is only one thing that you will need to worry about is the mold. Mold is an obvious growth – it is white, blue, or black fuzz that grows on top of the culture. All you need to do is toss the brew if you find any mold growing on it. If you have the necessary culture, and high-quality ingredients, you will be able to brew good kombucha.

Kombucha cures all

This is one thing you will need to remember – kombucha cannot be confused as a panacea. It does not cure anything, but detoxifies your body thereby ensuring the immune system functions well. You can think of this as a filter cleaner where the filter in this instance is your liver.

Kombucha has often been described as an adaptogen and satisfies the following criteria – it works on the whole body (nonspecific), helps the body maintain homeostasis, and is nontoxic. This means that kombucha can help you lose weight or gain weight depending on what your end goal is.

Chapter Four: How to Brew Kombucha

Now that we have learned what kombucha is and how it benefits you let us take a look at how to brew kombucha. This chapter also covers the mistakes that you must avoid when brewing kombucha and some tips that will make the brewing process easier.

Brewing Kombucha

Gathering the right equipment. It is easy to make kombucha at home and one needs only a few equipment to start. You will need the following:

- Wooden or Plastic stirring spoon
- Quart-sized glass jar, or bigger depending on the amount you want to brew
- Canning Jar rings or Rubber bands to secure the cover of the jar
- Paper Coffee filters or weave cloths

Most supplies can be found in any grocery store or in a DIY Kombucha Kit. It is best to purchase these kits if you are starting out since you will have all the necessary equipment, including the tea bottles, flavoring, and SCOBY.

Gather the Ingredients

The ingredients mentioned below are found in every starter pack or DIY kit. It is best to purchase this kit to make it easier on you. Once you get the hang of brewing kombucha, you can walk into any grocery store and purchase the necessary ingredients.

- Unchlorinated and unflouridated water
- Loose tea or tea bags (Green or Black Tea)
- White granulated or powdered sugar
- Active SCOBY
- Distilled White Vinegar or Starter Tea

You may be tempted to experiment with different types of vinegar, but it is important to use distilled white vinegar to provide the perfect acidic environment. Do not use rice vinegar or apple cider vinegar to make kombucha tea.

Once the SCOBY you have purchased becomes active, you can make kombucha using the ratios given below. You have to remember that the ratios are not for regular brewing. When your SCOBY is active for the first time, you must refer to the instructions that are provided in the instructions. If you have started making kombucha now, make small batches to maintain the proper ratios to avoid overworking the SCOBY.

Kombucha Ratios

These ratios will help you get started with making your first batch of kombucha.

One Quart:

- ¼ cup sugar
- 2 tea bags or 1 ½ tsp. loose tea
- 2 cups water
- ½ cup vinegar or starter tea

Half Gallon:

- ½ cup sugar
- 4 tea bags or 1 tbsp. loose tea
- 6 cups water
- 1 cup vinegar or starter tea

One Gallon:

- 1 cup sugar
- 8 tea bags or 2 tbsp. loose tea
- 13 cups water
- 2 cups vinegar or starter tea

Making the Tea

1. Boil the water and combine it with sugar in a glass jar. Stir the ingredients until the sugar has dissolved.
2. Add the tea bags or the loose tea to the jar and let the tea steep. You can contain the loose tea in a metal tea ball, but remember to remove the ball before you add SCOBY.
3. Let the mixture cool to 80 degrees Fahrenheit. It is better to leave the tea in the jar, since the tea will be stronger if the tea is left in the liquid for longer.

4. Remove the bags or the tea from the liquid and add the starter tea from a previous batch. If you are brewing for the first time, add the white vinegar to the liquid.
5. Remove any metal in the liquid and add some active SCOBY to the jar.
6. Cover the jar with using a coffee filter or weave cloth and secure it with a rubber band.
7. Leave the mixture in a cool dark place for at least 10 days before you taste. The longer the tea ferments, the more vinegary and less sweet it will taste.
8. Pour the kombucha from the top to consume and retain the tea and the SCOBY to use as starter tea for the next batch.
9. Bottle the kombucha after adding some flavor to it or enjoy it plain.

Common Mistakes made

Beginners are known to make a few mistakes when brewing kombucha for the first time. These mistakes can also be made by people who have brewing kombucha for some time.

Storing Kombucha in direct sunlight

It is important that you don't brew kombucha in direct sunlight. If you leave the jar in direct sunlight, the temperature within the jar may rise thereby creating an inhospitable environment for the yeast and bacteria that you are trying to grow. Brew the tea in a dark cupboard or in a room where there is no direct sunlight.

Rinsing SCOBY

Some brewers may want to rinse the SCOBY before adding it to tea like they would rinse tomatoes before adding them to a salad. It is important to remember to never rinse SCOBY since you will be washing away some of the microbial agents that are responsible for transforming the tea into kombucha. You can wash the SCOBY only if you drop it on the ground.

Refrigerating SCOBY

SCOBY consists of the mother culture that will help transform tea into kombucha. If you were to leave the SCOBY in the refrigerator, you would be damaging the fragile microorganisms in the SCOBY, thereby weakening the power of SCOBY. This SCOBY is likely to be contaminated with mold, or may produce kombucha that does not culture properly.

Using Weak Starter Tea

The SCOBY and tea are mixed together to transform the tea into kombucha. If you were to separate the SCOBY from the tea within six days, the kombucha is weak and cannot be used as starter tea for fresh brews. This will weaken your kombucha over time.

Oversteeping Tea

Tannins and other components in tea are released when you steep green or black tea in hot water. If tea is oversteeped, the flavor of the kombucha can become unpleasant and bitter.

Tips to Making Good Kombucha

Always use distilled water to avoid damaging your kombucha. Filters that are often used do not remove the impurities in the liquid.

You can share the starter tea between friends, but ensure that you and your friend are brewing the kombucha perfectly.

Refined table sugar is known to be bad for health, but this is the best sugar to use since the kombucha produces the best nutrients in this way. Most of the sugar has left the tea and the starter tea during the process of fermentation.

If you only use green tea to make kombucha, you should add one black tea bag would need to be used to give the kombucha the required amount of tannin.

Cool the tea for at least two hours to ensure that no mold is created during the fermentation process.

It is best to make kombucha in a bowl. You need to ensure that you select the right bowl to use. Avoid metal, except for stainless steel, or ceramic to prevent the leeching of toxins into the kombucha.

Chapter Three: Kombucha Recipes

Ginger and Blueberry Kombucha

This drink is both tangy and sweet. The trick to making this drink is to make the perfect ginger and blueberry sauce. You have to balance the flavors perfectly in this sauce to ensure that you have a zing in your tea.

Ingredients:

- 7 cups brewed kombucha (brewed)
- ½ cup blueberries
- 1 tbsp. lemon juice (freshly squeezed)
- ½ tbsp. honey
- ½ inch ginger (cut finely)

Directions:

1. Add the blueberries to a food processor and blend until smooth.
2. Next, add the lemon juice and ginger. Blend till there are no lumps in the mixture.
3. Add the honey to the processor. If you have brewed the kombucha for a longer period, you will need to add more honey to the processor to reduce the bitterness.
4. Blend all the ingredients till you obtain a smooth mixture. Transfer the mixture to the bottle and using a funnel, pour the kombucha into the bottle. Cap the bottle tightly and store in a cool place for a few hours or for as long as a day.
5. Refrigerate the bottles to stop the fermentation. When you are ready to drink the brew, pop a bottle open and enjoy.

Ginger and Lemon Kombucha

This brew would be good on hot days. The lemon, ginger, and honey create a fizzy brew that tastes lovely. You will forget about traditional lemonade when you begin to drink this brew.

Ingredients:

- 2 tsp. ginger, peeled and chopped
- 1 tbsp. lemon juice
- 1 tbsp. honey or sugar
- 3 cups kombucha (brewed)

Directions:
1. Add the ingredients, except for kombucha, to a bowl and mix well. If you are adding honey, take care to balance the flavors in the bowl.
2. Pour the kombucha into the bowl and cover it using an airtight lid. It is always safe to use bottles or airtight containers that are not plastic or metal.
3. Shake the mixture well and leave the bowl in a cool place for three days. If you find that the kombucha has fermented enough, place the bowl in the refrigerator to stop the fermentation process.
4. Uncover the bowl carefully without shaking it. This is to ensure that the kombucha does not spill over.
5. Strain the tea to remove the pieces of ginger. Serve it cold.

Chocolate and Strawberry Kombucha

If you are craving for a dessert fix, this is your go-to brew. The strawberry juice, cocoa powder, and kombucha blend well together to give you a lovely brew.

Ingredients:

- 32 ounces kombucha (brewed)
- 1 cup fresh strawberries
- 2 tsp. cocoa powder (unsweetened)
- 1 tsp. coconut sugar

Directions:

1. Extract the juice from the strawberry. Take two bottles and add a few strawberries and their juice in each.
2. Add the cocoa powder and the sugar to the bottle and shake well. It would be better to use ground sugar since that is easier to mix.
3. Fill both bottles with kombucha and cover with an airtight lid.
4. Leave the bottles in a cool place for five days before moving them to the refrigerator to stop the fermentation process.
5. Serve cold.

Virgin Mojito Kombucha

If you are looking for a mocktail brew, you should try the virgin mojito kombucha. This brew has the perfect blend of mint, sugar, and lemon juice, without the effects of alcohol.

Ingredients:

- 2 cups brewed kombucha
- 1 tsp. lime juice
- 1 sprig mint (fresh, washed, and dried)

Directions:
1. Choose the storage bottle and clean it with vinegar and hot water. Once the bottle has cooled and dried, prepare the ingredients you will need to use for the mojito.
2. Add all the ingredients, except for kombucha, to the bottle.
3. Remove the SCOBY from the brewed kombucha and set it aside for your next brew.
4. Pour the brewed kombucha into the glass bottle using a funnel. It is best to use a sieve to ensure that all lumps and stringy bits are removed from the brewed kombucha. Do not fill the bottle with a lot of kombucha since the bottle may explode during the process of fermentation.
5. Store the bottle in a cool place and leave the kombucha to ferment. Store the bottle in the refrigerator to stop fermentation.
6. Serve with ice.

Pumpkin Kombucha

You can enjoy this brew regardless of whether it is autumn or not. This brew has a meld of nutmeg and cinnamon with a hint of ginger that makes it a treat that you will not want to share.

Ingredients:

- 2 tsp. crushed ginger
- 1 tsp. nutmeg
- 1 cup pumpkin juice
- 1 tsp. powdered cinnamon
- 2 cups kombucha (brewed)
- 1 tbsp. honey

Directions:
1. Clean the bottle you will be using to brew your flavored kombucha.
2. Add the crushed ginger, nutmeg, cinnamon, and honey to the bottle. Mix the ingredients well.
3. Pour the pumpkin juice and shake the bottle well to mix all the ingredients. Taste the mixture and adjust the spice if necessary.
4. Add the kombucha to the bottle and cover it with an airtight lid.
5. Leave the bottle in a cool place and let it ferment for two days. If you prefer a less fermented drink, move the bottle to the refrigerator to stop the fermentation process.
6. Serve cold.

Cinnamon and Apple Kombucha

This brew tastes like sparkling apple cider vinegar and will be a favorite beverage in the fall. This slightly sweet, spicy and tangy brew is definitely worth the wait.

Ingredients:

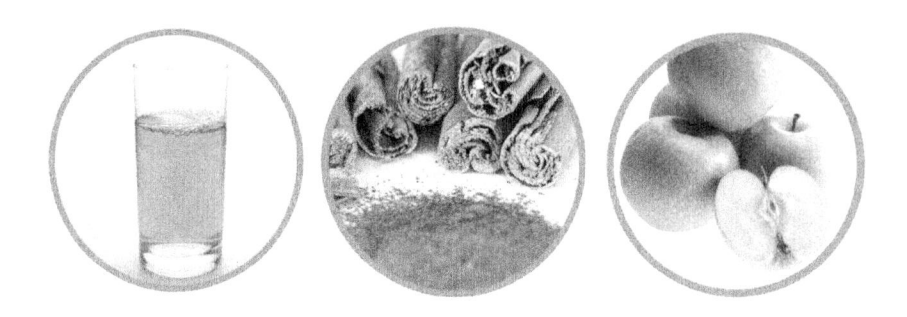

- 4 tbsp. fresh apple juice
- 1 tsp. cinnamon chips
- 2 cups kombucha (brewed)

Directions:

1. Mix the cinnamon chips and apple juice in a bottle and shake well.
2. Pour the brewed kombucha into the bottle leaving some space at the top. Cap the bottle tightly and leave the mix to ferment for three days or longer depending on your liking.
3. Strain the liquid to remove the cinnamon chips and drink.

Chia Seed Kombucha

Chia Seed kombucha is expensive when bought in the market, but you will spend only a third of the cost when you make this brew at home. You can enhance the kombucha using either dry seeds or the gel.

Ingredients:

- 1 tbsp. chia seeds or 2 tbsp. chia seeds gel
- 2 cups kombucha (brewed)

Directions:

1. Add the chia seeds or the gel to a bottle and top the chia seeds with kombucha.
2. Shake the bottle a little bit to ensure that the ingredients begin to blend. Continue to shake the bottle gently every few minutes.
3. Once the brew has gelled to your desired consistency, drink immediately or refrigerate.

Cayenne and Pineapple Kombucha

A pinch of cayenne pepper and pineapple mixed together make the perfect kombucha brew. You not only get the benefits of kombucha, but also the benefits of cayenne. The brew is a great way to aid in digestion.

Ingredients:

- 32 ounces kombucha (brewed and plain)
- 2 cups fresh pineapple
- ¼ tsp. cayenne pepper

Directions:

1. Cut the pineapple into thin slices, and add it to a food processor with one cup of kombucha and cayenne pepper. Blend the ingredients till you obtain a smooth mixture.
2. You can remove the pulp from the mixture if you like.
3. Add 2 ounces of the blended mixture to a bottle and fill the rest with kombucha. Leave some head space.
4. Cap the bottle with an airtight lid and shake gently.
5. Leave the bottle in a cool place for three days, after which you can move it to the refrigerator to store.

Basil with a Twist

This brew is refreshing and is a winner if you are looking to brew something with a twist. This is a little hard to make since you will need to wait a few days, but it is definitely worth the wait. You can add some vodka or rum if you want to make a killer cocktail!

Ingredients:

- 1 gallons kombucha (brewed)
- 2 cups fresh strawberries (chopped)
- 1 cup water
- 1 cup sugar
- 1 cup fresh basil (chopped)

Directions:

1. Set aside kombucha that is ready to be bottled.
2. Add the water, sugar, strawberries, and basil to a saucepan and bring the ingredients to a boil.
3. Simmer the ingredients in the pan for ten minutes while continuing to stir.
4. Mash the strawberries and leave the mixture in the refrigerator to cool.
5. Transfer the strawberry mixture to a bowl and add one cup of kombucha to it. Mix the ingredients well together.
6. Pour the mixture into a bottle and add the remaining kombucha to it. Leave some head space.
7. Cap the bottle tightly and leave it in a cool place for two to four days. If you prefer a lesser-fermented drink, leave the bottle in the refrigerator to stop the fermentation process.
8. Strain the kombucha in a glass, and drink cold.

Raspberry and Lemon Kombucha

This brew is a fizzy and delicious recipe that one must try. It is refreshing and is abundant with a lot of fruits. The brew will need to be fermented a second time to ensure that it is sweet enough. You can add sugar to the brew if you do not like the tartness of raspberries and lemons.

Ingredients:

- 3 ounces kombucha (brewed)
- 1 cup fresh raspberries (chopped)
- ½ tbsp. lime juice (freshly squeezed)
- Assorted fruits for garnish
- 1 tbsp. sugar (optional)

Directions:

1. If the brewed kombucha is tangy, you may need to add some sugar to the final brew. Try to ensure that the brew you use has the right balance. Set the SCOBY used aside.

2. If you are using bottles to make the brew, you can divide the raspberries and lemon juice equally among the bottles. Alternatively, if you are using a gallon container, you can add the raspberries and lime juice to the container.

3. Add the brewed kombucha to the bottles or the container and cover using an airtight lid.

4. Store the bottle in a cool place for one day. You can leave the containers for longer depending on how fermented you want the brew to be.

5. Refrigerate the containers to stop the fermentation process.

6. Serve cold with extra fruit.

Orange Kombucha

Ingredients:

- 2 ounces water
- 2 tsp. lime blossom loose tea
- 2 tsp. jasmine green loose tea
- 1 cup cane sugar
- ½ cup + 4 tsp. honey
- 2 tbsp. orange zest
- 2 tsp. orange juice

Directions:

1. Add lime blossom tea to hot water and let the tea steep for at least ten minutes. Now, add the jasmine tea and steep for fifteen minutes.

2. Strain the liquid and add the cane sugar and ½ of the honey. Mix the ingredients well together.

3. Transfer the mixture to a bottle and add all the other ingredients except for the kombucha to the bottle. Shake the bottle well and taste the blend. Balance the blend and add the kombucha to the bottle.

4. Cap the bottles tightly and store in a cool place. Leave the brew to ferment for three days and refrigerate.

5. Serve cold with a garnish of orange zest.

Conclusion

Thank you for purchasing the book.

Kombucha is a brew that is gaining popularity because of the multiple benefits it has to offer. Most people have started to brew kombucha at home, but only some of them are able to brew the perfect kombucha. This is because of some common mistakes that are made by people. Over the course of the book, you have learned what kombucha is, how to brew kombucha, and the mistakes to avoid making when brewing it.

I hope you have gathered all the information you need for kombucha.

Happy Brewing!

Once again, thank you for buying this book and good luck.

Printed in Great Britain
by Amazon